PREFACE

The purpose of *"INTERVIEW QUESTIONS"* is to enable you to understand the interview questions, answers, tips & techniques to get immediate hire. It brilliantly interprets what the interviewers want to hear and how to say it to them. The book, therefore, introduces you to understand what is behind the questions you'll be asked. No prior knowledge is required. I explore Job Interview, including its frontiers, in an easy-to-understand, user-friendly manner.

I hope that *"INTERVIEW QUESTIONS"* contributes to your understanding of the Job Interview market and imparts a sense of excitement in the process. You, the reader, are the final judge. I thank you for choosing this book.

AUTHOR

JAYANTA PRAMANIK

CONTENTS

INTERVIEW QUESTIONS

Interview Questions, Answers, Tips & Techniques to Get Immediate Hire

JOB INTERVIEWS

Great candidates being passed over because they didn't prepare for an interview properly. Even if you don't have the full skill set you can still land the job by being well prepared and enthusiastic.

Interviewers frequently test a candidate's preparation to see how enthusiastic they are about the role and the company. Thorough preparation demonstrates to them that you're serious about the job. The first thing to do is to visit the company's website and social channels. Make sure you read the company home page, latest news & services/product sections and note down the key points you learn about the company including its history, vision & mission. Then move on to a web search of the company to find out if it's been in the news lately. This will ensure you come across as informed and up-to-date with topical issues. It's also a good idea to know who its competitors are and what differentiates them from other businesses in their field.

Research Company Website

Go to the company website and find out what product or service they provide. How do they make money? Why does their client choose them?

Search for the Latest News

Go to the website and read some recent developments and press releases to get a sense of what the company is working on. The interviewer will be impressed with that if you know the recent developments and the latest news about them.

Social Media Accounts

Check the Company's Social Media Account (Twitter, LinkedIn, Facebook, Pinterest & Youtube) that gives you a feel about the company. You'll get a great sense of company culture and the type of people working there.

Industry & Competitor Research

Go to www.similarweb.com and research about the company. Try to find a few key differences and similarities, so you can show you understand the whole marketplace and industry, not just the company you're interviewing with. Hiring managers will be very impressed with this.

LinkedIn Research

Go to www.Linkedin.com and find people in the same type of group or role that you're interviewing for. What type of background do they have? Find out the trend for the type of person a company likes to hire.

The Hiring Manager

Go to google and research the Hiring Manager. You might see something you have in common with them. And if not, you'll still know more about them than most candidates going in for the interview. So it'll be easier to bond and build rapport.

YouTube

You can also look for the company on YouTube. Do a quick search and see if they have an account. More and more companies are doing this, so this is a worthwhile step in terms of how to research a company very thoroughly before you talk to them. You might also see their office in a video which will make you more comfortable when you arrive for an interview. You'll feel like you've been there before.

Connections

Do you know someone who works at the company? Ask them if they can help. If you're a college grad, ask your career office if they can give you a list of alumni who work there. Then email them, send a LinkedIn message, or call and ask for assistance.

Financial Health

While you're on the website, click on the "Investor Relations" tab. For most large companies, you should be able to access and listen to a publicly available quarterly earnings conference call and read an annual report. These calls and reports cover a range of topics, including new products, company risks, and whether revenues are growing or stable.

Make sure you can answer these questions about a company:

1. *Who is the CEO?*
2. *When/why was the company founded?*
3. *Do they have multiple locations?*
4. *How do they make money? What do they sell?*
5. *Why do their customers choose them?*
6. *How are they different from their competitors?*

Use that as a checklist to make sure you've researched the company enough before your interview.

JOB INTERVIEWS Q-A

Question: Why should we hire you?

INTENTION: The interviewer wants to know what makes you best fits for this position.

BEST ANSWER: For this particular job I have the right skills and knowledge that is required. My skills, knowledge, and interest combined with the history of getting results to make me valuable to your company. I have the ability to generate and promote growth, net positive income, and remarkable market return.

At the workplace I always try to be creative, bring in new ideas, and increase the profitability of the company.

Since I'd come from a new environment, I am bound to possess a new perspective towards everything here including the company, product, customer, services, strategies, and financial perspectives. This will enable me to constructively question and understand the things which anyone else here might not do. This will help improve things and to make the company better.

I prepared myself to be able for this job and I feel very confident of myself and my abilities to deliver nothing short of quality output.

So I believe my skills and work attitude measures up to your company standards.

## Question:	How do you think you can contribute to the job for which the interview you now?

INTENTION: The company wants to discover how you can help and what you'll be able to accomplish if you were to be hired.

BEST ANSWER: My skills and interest combined with the history of getting results to make me valuable to your company. For this particular job I have the right skills and knowledge that is required. I have the ability to generate growth, net positive income, and good market return.

Since I'm coming from the new environment, I bound to possess a new perspective towards everything here including company, product, service, customers, environment, strategy, etc.

This will enable me to constructively understand and question things which anyone else here might not do.

So my contribution will mostly be in the form of individually and that process I believe I can contribute a lot to your company.

Question: *What are your greatest strengths?*

INTENTION: The main reason interviewers ask this question is to identify how you feel about yourself. Do your strengths align with the needs of the company and the job's responsibilities? The company wants to learn whether you're a good fit for the role you're interviewing for.

BEST ANSWER: I'm a highly motivated person. I've never been afraid to keep going back until I get what I want. I'm smart, active, optimistic and very positive.

Question: What are your greatest weaknesses?

INTENTION: They try to find out whether you have a healthy level of self-awareness. Whether you pursue self-improvement and growth opportunities to combat these issues, as opposed to letting these weaknesses hold you back

BEST ANSWER: I sometimes push my people too hard. I like to work with a sense of urgency and everyone is not always on the same wavelength.

Question: Why do you want to work with us?

INTENTION: The interviewer wants to see your Enthusiasm for the position and the company. With a little forethought, your answer will help establish your credibility, convince a hiring manager to like you, and prove your value to an organization.

BEST ANSWER: The kind of development, work environment and employment facilities (benefits) you are offering that certainly help employees to perform at their best and work towards the organization's best.

I would be proud to work for a company like yours with such a good record & leadership in the industry. I've carried out my web research and believe that the company's service, products and future perspectives are very impressive and promising. Your company believes in providing quality and superior service to which I share the same value and where my skills or background fits perfectly and can be utilized respectively.

Question: Do you consider yourself successful?

INTENTION: The interviewer wants to know how you feel about yourself.

BEST ANSWER: I feel successful is a continuous process where I meet my short term as well as my long term goals. I try to reach those goals and achieve the desired outcome. I want to recognize myself as someone with a progressive attitude who does his best and gives a hundred percent to achieve his/her goals.

Question: Aren't you overqualified for this position?

INTENTION: Will you feel bored with your current job or you enjoy it? Will you leave your current employer as soon as something better comes your way? Anything you can say to demonstrate the sincerity of your commitment to the employer and encourage him that you're looking to stay for the long term

BEST ANSWER: I admit that I'm very well qualified for this position but I don't personally believe that I'm overqualified. For this particular post I have the best types of skills, knowledge, and expertise. I'm the type of person who does not become bored easily, simply because I am always been creative and looking for new things to do in the workplace.

There are many jobs that I could have applied for, but I chose this one because I want to work for your company and your team. I believe I can be a valuable asset in the post and the extra skills that I do have will hopefully be shared amongst my peers and the team.

Question: Where do you see yourself five years from now?

INTENTION: The reason behind the question is to see how well your answer lines up with the company's long term goals.

BEST ANSWER: In five years from now I want to see myself in a responsible position like a senior manager, where my company sees me as valuable assets and at the same time to grows with the company.

How long would you work here?

INTENTION: They want to see your level of engagement, and your enthusiasm for the position.

BEST ANSWER: Working in your company and particularly for this post was my dream. I prepared myself to be able for this job and I'm very serious about it.

I like new challenges and a chance to grow. As long as I keep getting these, I don't think I'll need to switch over. I'd like to believe that this relationship lasts for many years. However, I haven't set any time limit as such.

Question: How do you think you can contribute to the job for which the interview you now?

INTENTION: The hiring manager wants to hear in your own words how you feel you can be an asset to the company.

BEST ANSWER: My skills and interest combined with the history of getting results to make me valuable to your company. For this particular position I have the right type of skills and knowledge that is required. I have the ability to generate growth, net positive income, and good market return. Since I'm coming from the new environment I bound to possess a new perspective towards everything here including company, product, service, customer, environment, strategy, etc.

This will enable me to constructively understand and question things which anyone else here might not do.

So, I think my contribution will mostly be in the form of individually and that process I believe I can contribute a lot to your company.

Question: What are your career objectives?

INTENTION: The interviewer wanting to know if the job will be a good fit given your projected career path. Does it make sense given your long-term career strategy? Will you stick around in the position for a reasonable amount of time? Are your ambitions reasonable, and in line with the company?

BEST ANSWER: I've learned that long term goals are best achieved when I break them into short term goals. My long term goal is to settle myself in a responsible position in your organization, like a senior manager, where my company sees me as a valuable asset and at the same time to grow with the company. My short term goal is to find a place in your company where I can promote growth, net positive income, and good market return.

## Question:	How do you compensate for your lack of experience?

INTENTION:	Keep in mind that lack of experience does not mean an immediate disqualification from the job. Most interviewers ask questions of experience, or lack thereof, in order to gauge how a candidate reacts to a direct challenge.

BEST ANSWER: I have the ability to learn and grasp things quickly. Every time there is something new to me, I take the time to study it the soonest time. I'm already telling you that I'm a highly motivated person. I have never been afraid to keep going back until I get what I want.

## Question:	Are you applying to other jobs as well?

INTENTION: Primarily, the hiring manager wants to know if the interviewee takes the job search process seriously and plans on applying for more than one position to increase the chances of obtaining meaningful employment.

BEST ANSWER: Yes, I have submitted my application in some of the best companies like (mention the company you already applied to) Amazon, Google, Walmart, Verizon. Above all, my priority and hope are that I'm able to land a job in your company.

Question: Have you ever worked in a job that does not match your skills?

INTENTION: To assess how reliable and agreeable of an employee you are, an interviewer may ask if you have ever experienced a job without matching skills and, if so, how you handled the situation. Most employees will experience problems with a supervisor at some point, and this question lets an interviewer understand how you are inclined to handle that common situation.

BEST ANSWER: I once had a job that does not exactly match my qualifications. Nevertheless, I was glad, I took the job because it was an excellent opportunity to learn something new and added to my list of experiences.

Question: Do your skills match this job or another job more closely?

INTENTION: The interviewer wants to see the qualifications that only you can offer.

BEST ANSWER: I feel my skills are the best fit for this job.

Question: If you were hiring a person for this job, what would you look for?

INTENTION: The hiring manager is seeing what you find important. That will tell them what qualities you will strive to bring to the table. It will also show what you would appreciate seeing in co-workers. Do you think attitude trumps ability? Do you think written communication is as valuable as verbal?

BEST ANSWER: I would look into two essential things: (1) The ability to do the job right and (2) The proper attitude to do it. Skills without the right attitude will not contribute to productive output.

Question: Why do you think you would do well at this job?

INTENTION: The interviewer wants to focus on your interests and reasons for pursuing the position. He is looking to see if you are truly enthusiastic about the job, but also evaluating your qualifications and whether it seems like you would do well in the position.

BEST ANSWER: This job is something which is my interest. I prepared myself to be able for this job and I love to do it. I feel very confident about myself and my ability to deliver nothing short of quality output. My skills and experience helped me to develop this confidence.

Question: Why should we hire you?

INTENTION: Hiring managers use job interviews to ultimately determine whether they should offer you a job. To glean the information they need to make that decision.

BEST ANSWER: For this particular job I have the right skills that are required. I have strong (Name the skills that you have) communication skills, multitasking skills, coding skills, lead generation skills, leadership skills.

So, I believe my skills and work attitude measures up to your company standards.

Question: Are you willing to travel?

INTENTION: When the hiring manager asks this question, they are looking to gauge your willingness to travel—and the extent to which you will travel for the job. Often, the hiring manager will explain the travel requirements for the job during your interview, after you answer the question regarding willingness. The hiring manager will share their expectations with you so that you can decide whether or not the position is a good fit for you.

BEST ANSWER: Yes, I love traveling. Adjusting to new places and meeting new people would be a delightful experience for me.

Question: Tell me about your dream job?

INTENTION: There are two reasons why interviewers ask the question "What is your dream job?" **Firstly**, to get an idea of your passions, values and motivations as an employee. Will you be satisfied with the position if you got the job offer. **Secondly**, the prospective employer is trying to figure out if you have the skills necessary to do the job.

BEST ANSWER: The dream job I have always had was a job that keeps me positive, motivates me to continue; a job wherein I get to contribute to the company's success.

Question: Why did you leave your last job?

INTENTION: Hiring managers really want to know if you left voluntarily or for a good reason. If you left on good terms, this paints you in a favorable light. Your reasons for moving on can say a lot about your values as an employee.

BEST ANSWER: I left my previous job because I feel I want to do more, to get hold of a greater opportunity to serve.

Question: What experience do you have in this field?

INTENTION: What they are really asking is what type of experience do you expect proper candidates to have, and in turn, what type of employee are you seeking. If their skills do not match what you state, they may question if the position would be a good fit for them.

BEST ANSWER: I've proficient and extensive knowledge in (tell your experience) coding, business management, sales management, lead generation, cash flow analysis, multitasking, etc.

Besides, I'm an expert in certain strategies (tell the interviewer if you have strong knowledge if any).

Question: What co-workers say about you?

INTENTION: The interviewer is really trying to decide if you will fit in with their company environment. Not every individual will be able to succeed in their company climate, it is your job to convince the interviewer that you are one of the proper candidates.

BEST ANSWER: They say that I'm extremely persistent. I've never been afraid to keep going back until I get what I want. They also say I'm a hardworking, patient and quick learner.

Question: How would you know you were successful in this job?

INTENTION: The interviewer wants to know how would you judge yourself.

BEST ANSWER: I think success refers to a continuous process when I meet my short term as well as my long term goals. I try to reach those goals and achieve the desired outcome.

I would recognize myself as someone with a progressive attitude who does his best and gives a hundred percent to attain goals.

For this particular job, I have the right skills and knowledge that are required (gives a brief description of your knowledge and skills). Apart from that this job is something which is my interest. I prepared myself to be able for this job and I love to do it.

I feel very confident in myself and my abilities to deliver nothing short of quality output. My skills and experience help me to develop this confidence.

Question: How would you be an asset to this company?

INTENTION: The Interviewer wants to know what they will get out of the deal. He is only, or primarily, concerned with how their company will benefit from hiring you.

BEST ANSWER: My skills and interest combined with the history of getting the result make me valuable to your company. I have the ability to promote and increase growth, market return, net positive income and the bottom line of the company. At the workplace, I try to do the very best that I'm capable of; I always try to be creative, bring in new ideas and increase the overall profitability.

As an employee, I think my skills, knowledge and attitude measures up to your company standards and make me a valuable asset to this company.

Question: Why do you think you would do well at this job?

INTENTION: The interviewer wants to see if there's anything unique about you that'll help you perform well in the job.

BEST ANSWER: This job is something which is my interest. I prepared myself to be able for this job and I love to do it. I feel very confident in myself and my abilities to deliver nothing short of quality output. My skills and experience help me to develop this confidence. So I think I would do well at this job.

Question: What is the most difficult decision for you made?

INTENTION: The interviewer wants to find out both what you consider to be your hardest decision and how you made the decision. Although the question is only asking about the decision itself, the interviewer will typically drill down into the details around what led up to the need to make the decision, the process you went through for the decision and the eventual outcome and fallout as a result of the decision.

BEST ANSWER: It was a time when I had to choose between joining a group of employees protesting some issues in the company, and staying away from the issue. I ended up being a mediator between the employees and our immediate supervisor. I was glad I made that decision because it all ended well and without further conflicts in the workplace.

Question: What qualities do you look for in a boss?

INTENTION: The purpose of this question is to determine whether you will fit for the managerial framework of this company or not. It also tells them in which office environment you would be working best.

BEST ANSWER: I look into my boss as a person who can easily relate with me, can make firm decisions and is transparent. A boss with a sense of humor would also be a delightful idea.

Question: Do you know anyone who works in our company?

INTENTION: The Interviewer would like to see if a friend referred you to this position, a former co-worker, or an industry acquaintance. This question is another way of the interviewer asking where you heard about the role, and if you have any connections from within.

BEST ANSWER: (1) Tell the interviewer if you know anyone in the company or (2) I do not personally know anyone who works for your company; however, I am connected with a couple of your employees on LinkedIn due to common group interest. I look forward to getting to know your team!

Question: What suggestions have you made in your previous employment that was implemented?

INTENTION: The purpose of this question is to gain insight into your mindset, including your priorities and values in the workplace. If you recognize this, you can spend time thinking about what aspects the interviewer is likely looking for. Which will allow you to incorporate these elements into your answer?

BEST ANSWER: I once suggested that management and staff should have more regular meetings instead of quarterly meetings. I was happy that management took note of this and even commended me for making a good initiative.

Question: What are your career options right now?

INTENTION: The interviewer wants to see how you can position yourself as a desired candidate.

BEST ANSWER: Right now my career option is to work for a company like yours with such a good record in the industry, and become an integral part of the company. At the same time I want to use my knowledge and skills to achieve growth, positive income, and good market return.

Question: Would you rather work for money or job satisfaction?

INTENTION: The interviewer is looking for your decision-making capabilities.

BEST ANSWER: Job satisfaction is more important to me. Working just for the money is not desirable if I don't like the job in the first place. Job satisfaction makes you stay productive; money would naturally come along well.

Question: What were your biggest challenges with your previous superiors?

INTENTION: The interviewer wants to assess how reliable and agreeable of an employee you are, an interviewer may ask if you have ever experienced issues with a supervisor and, if so, how you handled the situation.

BEST ANSWER: My previous superiors were very disciplined and strict when it comes to deadlines and output. It was a challenge for me to meet every expectation they made. It was also a good learning experience for me because it only made me better at what I do.

Question: How do you plan to achieve your career goals?

INTENTION: The interviewer may also want to know how your goals relate to working at the company if you were to be hired. Do your goals mesh with a career path at the company, or will they take you to a different occupation or industry?

BEST ANSWER: In the next five years I want to develop my intuitive understanding of the industry and start to build my client base.

My long term plan is to have a strong relationship with my colleagues and clients in addition to having my own business. However, before that happens, I want to get experience at a firm like yours, with such a good record in the industry.

Question: In what area do you need to improve your skills?

INTENTION: This question is designed to find out how you view yourself and your opportunities for growth. It can also be asked to get a feel for your priorities. In other words, are you interested in improving yourself more in a personal or professional capacity?

BEST ANSWER: Well, I'm working on improving some project management and organizational tools and technologies right now. As I take on more and more manageable in my career, I've realized if I become an expert in project management software and programs like Excel, it will make me even more productive. So I'm trying to go from 'good' to 'great' in this area.

I'd like to improve every facet of my life. No matter how much I may excel at a particular skill or task, I believe I can always get better and would like an opportunity to gain new experiences that will help me become better at anything I undertake. Does your company offer any extended training courses that I can take advantage of?

Question: Did you have any problem finding our office?

INTENTION: The interviewer usually asks this question to make the candidate cozy and comfortable.

BEST ANSWER: It was quite easy to find this place.

Question: How are you today?

INTENTION: This shows that the interviewer is quite caring and polite. He or she wants to put the candidate to ease before getting down to serious business.

BEST ANSWER: I am very well. Thank You.

Question: Tell me something about your values. What are your work ethics?

INTENTION: When a hiring manager asks you questions about your work style, what they are really asking is how well you would fit in with the company culture and the job itself. While it may seem as if the employer is trying to determine whether or not you are a hard worker, they are really trying to decide whether you are a team player. If you are not, are you willing to adapt and partake in collaborative initiatives as the job demands?

BEST ANSWER: I always try to do the very best that I'm capable of since my employer is paying me for it. At work I always want to be creative, bring in new ideas and increase the overall profitability of the company. I like to work the best that I can deliver.

Question: What is your management style?

INTENTION: The interviewer wishes to know whether someone who is joining at a lower level has the potential to manage a team.

BEST ANSWER: I believe that a manager's job is to balance company goals with worker satisfaction in order to make operation as efficient and profitable as possible. A good manager must also try to anticipate problems before they happen and in order to accomplish this, one can not be a dictator or distant and reserved form his subordinates, as they will not be properly motivated to assist in this process.

Question: Your Idea of an Ideal company?

INTENTION: Your interviewer wants to know why you've chosen to apply for a job at this firm over all of your other available options. You are being asked what it is about this company that makes it a good fit for your aspirations, values, skills, and priorities.

BEST ANSWER: An Ideal company provides maximum opportunity for the growth of employees. They provide a comfortable and flexible work environment so that employees can perform at their best and work towards companies best.

Question: What do you do to improve your knowledge?

INTENTION: How you keep yourself abreast of the new developments in your industry.

BEST ANSWER: To improve my knowledge I read books, journals, magazines, browse websites and often attain seminars. EBooks are a potential source of knowledge, I read EBooks to improve my knowledge.

Question   Where do you want to see yourself in five years?

INTENTION: The interviewer wants to know more about your career goals and how this position would fit into your grand plan. They care about your career goals because they want to hire someone who is motivated, proactive, and likely to stick around and work hard if hired.

BEST ANSWER: I hope to be working with your company as a senior manager, achieving great results in my department in five years' time.

Question: What is your strategy in the coming days?

INTENTION: This question is somewhat straightforward, as the interviewer does wish to know if you have an approach in mind, should you be hired. However, it's likely that he or she does not actually wish to hear the plan in great detail; your answer has more to do with your mindset and qualifications.

BEST ANSWER: I'll use my initial days in understanding my role carefully in terms of the contribution to the business and increase the overall profitability.

I'll sit with my line manager and other juniors to understand what has already been done and what its impact has been.

Question: Any questions for me?

INTENTION: The interviewer usually asks this question to make the candidate easy and comfortable.

BEST ANSWER: Could you please describe the work culture.

Question: How do you think you can contribute to the job for which the interview is now?

INTENTION: Interviewers ask questions like this to assess how well you understand the job responsibilities, as well as what you know about the company. And they also want to know how you will help make the company more successful or profitable.

BEST ANSWER: Although I do think I technically qualified for the job my contribution will mostly be in the form of individually and that process I believe It will be a lot of learning experience for me. In the initial time I'll sit with my manager and my peers to see what has already been done and what it's impact has been.

Most importantly I have the ability to identify problems and use my experience and energy to solve them. I want to create new things, bring in new ideas and increase overall profitability. So, I think in that process I can contribute a lot.

Question: How long do you expect to stay with our organization?

INTENTION: This question is usually asked to uncover those people who move between jobs frequently. Since the hiring process costs a lot, companies are looking for those who plan on staying for a long time. Companies that are looking for long-term employees aren't likely to be impressed with those who only want a job that they'll leave within a few months.

BEST ANSWER: I like new challenges and a chance to grow. As long as I keep getting these, I don't think I'll need to switch over. I'd like to believe that this relationship will last for many years. However I haven't set any time limit as such.

Question: What are the most important things as a manager?

INTENTION: Employers want to see your management style, strategic planning.

BEST ANSWER: The most important thing as a manager to me is (1) My team is quite happy and a good performing team. (2) The project I'm working on with my team is successfully finished with minimum problems.

Question: What do you do in your spare time?

INTENTION: The interviewer determines if a new hire will suit the existing company culture. How people choose to have fun impacts on how they'll work with an established team of employees.

BEST ANSWER: In my spare time I like to make sure that I keep myself occupied in some creative ways. I enjoy playing Guitar. I like to stay sharp by reading Books, Journals, and solving mathematical problems.